THE LANGUAGE OF LEADERS

A ROADMAP TOWARD EXCELLENCE

Dr. Eugene L. Moore, MBA

The Language of Leaders,
A Roadmap Toward Excellence
By Eugene L. Moore, Copyright 2022
ISBN: 978-1-947288-68-3

All rights reserved solely by the author. Except where designated, the author certifies that all contents are original and do not infringe upon the legal rights of any other person. No part of this book may be reproduced in any form without permission in writing from the publisher, except in the case of brief quotations embodied in critical articles or reviews.

10 9 8 7 6 5 4 3 2 1

Printed in the United States of America

Cover design by: Treviante Brown

Back cover photo by: Gies College of Business

Published by: Life To Legacy, LLC
P.O. Box 1239
Matteson, IL 60443
877-267-7477
www.Life2Legacy.com

Contents

About the Author	4
Acknowledgments	8
Foreword I	10
Foreword II	13
Preface	18
Introduction	20
1. Listen	25
2. Educate	30
3. Act	35
4. Delegate	40
5. Excite	45
6. Reflect	49
7. Showoff	54
Conclusion	58

About the Author

IT has been nearly three years since Dr. Eugene L. Moore, MBA, published his sixth book titled *The Business in You: Unleashing the Entrepreneur*, that provided tangible skills that an aspiring or existing business owner can use to assess their business idea or current model. The global pandemic has created and exposed many disparities; however, it has equally caused many individuals to reach into the depths of their creative prowess to build a successful business. I and society, have equally seen people utilize the gig economy to earn additional income to support their families. Whether they aligned with DoorDash, UberEats, GrubHub, Instacart, or another company; they quickly realized some components of entrepreneurship. In fact, there have been many stories throughout the pandemic where individuals started in a gig job that later morphed into a creation of a new business. According to the Census Bureau, more than 4.4 million new businesses were created in 2020. These realities, coupled with a more than 20-year history in the business sector and higher education, inspired his latest book, titled *The Language of Leaders: A Roadmap Toward Excellence*. While starting a business is inherently challenging, it can also be difficult leading a group of individuals in a work environment. Thus, Dr. Moore wanted to lend his expertise around what it means to be an effective leader, and to expand his leadership, he obtained certifications from the University of South Florida-Muma School of Business and the prestigious Harvard University. These certifications provided him with the skills needed to secure diversity, equity, and inclusion (DEI) in the workplace coupled with utilizing business strategy to solve complex problems. As a transformational leader, Dr. Moore is committed to move diversity beyond tolerance and compliance. He believes in order for diversity to be sustainable it needs to have a P.U.L.S.E. (People Uniting Long-term to Strengthen Everyone). When a leader applies this level of commitment, it will foster true diversity and enhance their leadership, learning, and legacy.

He firmly believes leaders are keenly receptive to learning and spend a great deal of time reading relevant materials and listening to other experts. He believes a great leader is always asking themselves and others, "How do we strategically and proactively prepare ourselves for things that have not yet transpired and what can we do to improve our ability to effectively lead others?" One of the biggest mistakes people make is believing leadership is a top-down ideology. While it is widely known that Jeff Bezos is the founder of Amazon, it should not be assumed that his innovative genius and leadership abilities are the sole rationale for how and why the company has been afforded such an enormity of success because such an assumption would be far-reaching. Dr. Moore has been quoted saying, "You do not have to hold a leadership position to be a leader, but you can lead wherever you find yourself in the organization by finding a solution to a problem." Effective leaders foster an environment where everyone believes that they can contribute to the growth and development of the company. Companies like Google or Microsoft cannot have sustainability if they are only relying on the innovative genius of their leaders. They must hire and retain talented individuals who inherently understand that leadership is not solely housed in the C-Suite.

In addition to working for the University of Illinois, he serves as the President and Chief Executive Officer of Assurance Creek Youth Program, Inc. and as a consultant to various global business enterprises. His latest book serves as an example of his commitment to using his gifts, talents, and resources to help others. Dr. Moore firmly believes that while education is knowledge, wisdom is power and if you desire for that power to have a compounded effect you must share it with as many people as possible. He will continue to use his platform to inspire the next generation of leaders and encourage them to pay it forward.

Acknowledgments

I am deeply grateful for a life of good health, a strong upbringing, a mother who demanded excellence and a grandmother who helped to shape my character. My educational attainment has been life changing but I am aware of the countless others who were not afforded such a reality. No amount of education, international travel, or a high-profile position will ever allow me to forget those who were systematically pushed aside and told it was solely due to their lack of effort. Meritocracy is not why I succeeded because I know that there are many individuals who work harder than I ever will, but my success is contingent upon boldly confronting a lie that was told to me which unashamedly stated, "I would not succeed." I have used every failure and every closed door as a teachable moment. I no longer stand outside of a closed door feeling defeated but instead pivot rather quickly thanking God for the protection of the unknown. I cannot orchestrate which rooms I must enter but I do know wherever I find myself I will demonstrate leadership. When I have had direct reports or when I was leading from the sidelines, I never forgot that each employee enters the office space with varied experiences. I do not know the details of their lives per say but I do want them to know I always leave room for anyone to seek comfort in my presence. I project empathy and a high sense of emotional intelligence so that everyone knows they can be their authentic self without judgment or ridicule. Whether we acknowledge it or not we are all seeking to be loved, appreciated, and respected and when we do not see that in our leaders it makes work more daunting and less joyous. The notion that we must hate our jobs or bosses is ludicrous, but it is also telling as it indicates our inherent cynicism. For those leaders in my career who led with disdain, micromanagement, anger, a lack of empathy, and unprofessionalism, I am truly grateful. Those leaders provided me with tangible evidence of what poor leadership entails which inspired me to lead with excellence and compassion, and for that, I say thank you.

Foreword I

WHILE I have led in various aspects of my life, one of the most memorable experiences was in 2015 when I served as the Cadet Battalion Commander for my high school, Chicago Military Academy in Bronzeville. Within this role, my team consisted of an Executive Officer (XO), operational staff, and Cadet Judge Advocate General. The XO can be considered the Chief of Staff who is charged with supporting drive, strategy, and enthusiasm. In conjunction with the XO and my team, we were responsible for the weekly operations of over five hundred students. As we navigated our academic journey and extracurricular activities, there were several pieces to the puzzle. However, being seen as a student leader was a key indicator of our success.

Early adoption of leadership skills can result in long-term name recognition, empowerment, and significant impact. Dr. Eugene Moore in his 2022 book *The Language of Leaders: A Roadmap Towards Excellence* illustrates seven principles that are practical to ensure your organization cultivates a team-winning culture. Ranging from the Cadet Battalion Commander to my current role as a Customer Success Account Manager at Microsoft, leadership is a transferable skill that impacts my daily performance. Dr. Moore speaks on how leadership takes the skills to confirm that individuals feel seen and heard. The ability to hear your team helps to ensure care, empathy, and compassion are at the forefront.

Leaders are filled with curiosity. Curiosity helps to explain one's understanding of systems, to provide a unique perspective towards innovation. Within *The Language of Leaders: A Roadmap Towards Excellence*, the reader will understand the power of a growth mindset. The ability to think BIG and in-depth ideas of exploration reap long-term benefits for teams. Thinking BIG is not the final step. One must make decisions from their ideation to move forward. Acting on the ideas, and reviewing previous paths, are essential toward an organization's growth. One may argue that looking back will cause you to encounter similar disappointments in the future. Thus, it is recommended to never look back and keep your eyes ahead. Dr. Moore provides a unique explanation on the importance of understanding the lessons, from our past, in our journey to becoming effective and successful. The lesson here helps to deliver the message that failure is not fatal, instead a learning opportunity.

In today's virtual world, team excitement is critical towards performance and the reduction of burnout. Dr. Moore highlights how a leader can excite their team to understand the company's mission towards one goal: success. From the new hire with no work experience to the senior level staff preparing for retirement, excitement is diverse, yet it's important to exist in your organization. At Microsoft, leaders are charged with exhibiting a mental approach which focuses on three key factors which are model, coach, and care. This strategy is undergirded by a growth mindset which allows leaders to model desired behaviors, coach their teams on how to demonstrate the desired behavior, and most importantly, showcasing their care for their team's continual growth. Hence, effective leaders are willing to show up with their team, feel their pain points, display empathy in action, and provide motivation when KPIs (Key Performance Indicators) may not be aligned with expectations.

A leader is not solely defined by a title, but is someone who reflects desired behaviors, actions, and characteristics that move their organization in a positive direction. After reading *The Language of Leaders: A Roadmap Towards Excellence*, the reader will gain an understanding of the skills needed to help drive team performance and foster a work culture of growth. Thank you, Dr. Moore, for your guidance on steps leaders should take toward excellence.

—Steven J. Williams III, MBA
Microsoft

Foreword II

I am honored to write this foreword for this very timely book. As we begin 2022, the challenges presented by the COVID pandemic remain with us. The global supply chain has been negatively impacted, and companies cannot deliver on planned purchases. The pandemic has led to what has been termed a labor mismatch, where demand for labor has outstripped supply as companies are faced with labor force attrition. Private-sector wages have increased at more than double the long-term pre-COVID growth rates, yet positions remain unfilled. Some of these shifts and other changes caused by the pandemic are most certainly temporary, but others could have a longer-lasting impact on how we conduct business. As companies seek to emerge from this era of lockdowns and market uncertainty, today's leaders will need to look forward and imagine new ways of steering their companies rather than look to old playbooks for solutions.

The Language of Leaders: A Roadmap Towards Excellence, plays a vital role in challenging the old ways of doing business. Dr. Eugene Moore outlines a path forward for leaders—whether you are in the C-Suite, a small start-up, or managing a small team in an organization. This book identifies specific skills that could be learned by anyone who has been asked to lead. Skills that are actionable and could be developed and enhanced through practice. He encourages existing and aspiring leaders to listen to your team; educate yourself and others; act deliberately—don't hesitate; delegate tasks strategically; excite your team so that they are motivated to get the job done; reflect the values that you desire from your team and respectfully show off your team's accomplishments.

These principles are clear signposts for you to follow as you take the leadership path. Adhering to these guidelines could enhance your chances of success as a leader, whereas failing to do so could result in a breakdown in trust, loss of empathy, and a lack of psychological safety for employees. Both anecdotal evidence and scientifically collected data support this.

When I completed my MBA in 1995, I worked for a medium-sized advertising agency in New York City. Our firm managed effective and popular advertising efforts like the *Milk Moustache* campaign. One of our clients was a well-known drug manufacturer who had manufactured a drug for a specific ailment but realized that one of the side effects of this drug was it lowered cholesterol levels for patients. I was tasked with developing a white paper that examined the consumer response to advertising this drug as a cholesterol reducer. I conducted focus groups and administered numerous surveys. My conclusion—patients would not take a medication that was difficult to tolerate when consuming for a largely asymptomatic ailment. Even if they started to take it, they would be less likely to adhere to the regimen and purchase refills, given that they would feel no different when they stop or start taking their medicine. My extensive report recommended that the company cease this effort to position this drug as a cholesterol-reducing medication. The leadership in the agency ignored these recommendations. The pharmaceutical company moved forward and lost a substantial amount of money in the effort.

This was a prime example of poor leadership. My voice was not heard, and my recommendations were ignored. No longer did I believe in the leadership at my agency. They did not listen, nor did they act on my findings. This led to a breakdown in trust and a lack of psychological safety.

Trust is critical in the workplace. If your team members do not trust you, they will doubt your intentions and capabilities. They may also question their own ability to adapt and respond to a rapidly changing environment. This is especially true post-COVID, where employees are tasked with accomplishing objectives with fewer resources at their disposal. Effective leadership requires that you inspire trust from others; this occurs when employees know that you trust them—their opinions and their jobs. Listening to your employees and acting on their recommendations are critical steps in this process of developing a trusting relationship.

Another important outcome of following Dr. Moore's signposts is an empathetic relationship with your employees. When you listen to employees, reflect on the desired values, and show off your team's accomplishments, employees will know that you care about them and their opinions. Empathy allows leaders to build and develop relationships with those they lead, and it is important for everything from innovation to retention. Research at the University of Illinois found that when employees perceive a lack of empathy at work, they tend to experience negativity that spills over into their personal lives, particularly with their partners. In addition, a study published in the *Academy of Management Journal* found that their performance could suffer; they are less likely to help others leading to poor customer service and higher turnover.

Finally, these steps outlined by Dr. Moore could lead to a sense of psychological safety. Employees feel valued, and they are not afraid to express their opinions even though they may not align with the status quo. Psychological safety is rooted in the idea that an employee won't be punished or embarrassed for speaking up with ideas, questions, concerns—even if they are not fully formed and are counter to conventional company practice. In a 2018 Gallup poll, 30% of employees surveyed stated that they did not feel comfortable speaking up at work.

When psychological safety exists, employees are not afraid to take risks. Organizations are more innovative, agile and respond more positively to change. In her book, *The Fearless Organization: Creating Psychological Safety in the Workplace for Learning, Innovation, and Growth*, Dr. Amy Edmondson, stated that "people must be allowed to voice half-finished thoughts, ask questions out of left field, and brainstorm out loud to create a culture that truly innovates."

Effective leadership plays a pivotal role in creating an organization built on trust, empathy and creates a space of psychological safety. People do not care what you know until they know that you care.

Dr. Moore's conceptual signposts guide leaders to this place. If leaders listen, educate, act, delegate, excite their team, reflect the values, and show off their team, then their employees will trust them, be more committed, innovative, and loyal to their team and organization.

—Hayden Noel, Ph.D.
Clinical Professor
Gies College of Business
University of Illinois at Urbana-Champaign

Preface

IT is arguably true that leadership is an essential component of a successful business, but I would imagine we all have worked for companies or institutions where the leadership was poor, but the overall organization was performing well. Perhaps these woes are at the mid-management level where the managers are less skilled than the C-Suite executives. Nonetheless, these realities exist and cause major tension within an organization. I would contend having a successful business model is great but if your employees do not feel valued you will be constantly hiring new employees. I am certain these continual vacancies will surely have some impact on profit. When we lose employees especially good ones, we lose their human capital which has proven to be detrimental to an organization ranging from their brand value to their recruitment efforts.

It is unwise to believe an attractive compensation package can deflect poor leadership. *The Language of Leaders: A Roadmap Toward Excellence* hopes to provide readers with useful and practical strategies to develop or enhance their leadership ability. In interviews prospective candidates will often ask the question, "What is your leadership style?" While this is a commonly asked question and perhaps only a small percentage of candidates want to know the truth, it does indicate that leadership is a key component to understanding an organization on a deeper and practical level. For example, companies like Nike, Tesla, Rolex, and countless others have created phenomenal brands but how does it look to work for these companies. Therefore, understanding leadership should not be a trivial question in an interview, but prospective employees should truly interrogate the response to ensure they are accepting a new position that aligns with their needs for a leader. This book is not designed to be an all-inclusive manual for leadership but hopefully serves as another tool to enhance your leadership abilities.

Introduction

WHAT is leadership? While the question seems simple it can certainly have varied meanings based upon who is defining the term. According to the Merriam-Webster dictionary leadership is defined as "a position as a leader of a group, organization, etc." Furthermore, they define a leader as, "a person who has commanding authority or influence." The mere definition of a leader gives us all access to become one irrespective of where we are positioned in an organization.

Famed psychologist Kurt Lewin is mostly identified by his contribution of the three most practiced leadership styles. Lewin led a group of researchers in the late 1930s to study which leaderships styles were most favored by participants as it related to their performance. The three types of leadership according to Lewin are autocratic, democratic, and laissez-faire. Now more than 80 years after Lewin's study there are many variations of the top leadership styles. Hence, the popular employment website for jobs, Indeed, Inc. listed the top ten common leadership styles which are coach, visionary, servant, autocratic, laissez-faire, democratic, pacesetter, transformational, transactional, and bureaucratic. The purpose of this book is not to debate which leadership style is the most effective, but it aims to improve your overall ability to lead others in the most productive and effective manner. In my opinion debating over which leadership style is most effective would be counterproductive because it forces us to deal with the ideology of the style of leadership and not the individual(s) who are responsible for working with others to produce favorable outcomes. Thus, this book focuses on what it takes to be an effective leader irrespective of the style they choose to use to demonstrate their leadership. The book offers a seven-step strategy to be an effective leader in any business setting.

First, a leader must have an exceptional ability to *Listen* effectively. In fact, they should understand what it means to be an active listener as they must contend with the daily opinions and suggestions of various stakeholders.

Secondly, they must be unyielding in their ability to *Educate* themselves and others. Your team must understand your desire to be an expert not someone who is arrogant or pretentious but someone who desires to feed their team with the most current and informative knowledge. Additionally, an effective leader encourages their team to continually seek professional development because knowledge needs to flow from and towards the leader.

Thirdly, as a leader you must *Act* in a deliberate and

pragmatic way so that your team finds confidence in your ability to lead with precision. To act is not always an easy thing for some leaders but it is proven that leaders who demonstrate this behavior are more respected by their peers as most people do not like passive-aggressive leaders who often hide behind others.

Fourth, great leaders learn how to masterfully *Delegate* tasks and not merely to just unload work onto others but to allow people to work within their potential and beyond.

Fifth, great leaders can naturally *Excite* their team and even when frustration persists it is never at the expense of not being motivated to fulfill the mission and vision of the company.

Sixth, a leader must *Reflect* the values they desire to see in others. It is a difficult task to move others toward excellence when you are content with mediocre outcomes and characteristics for yourself.

Lastly, a great leader is a *Showoff* and while I know one's inclination is that a showoff is an undesirable trait, I assert it is not when you are showing off the talents of your team. Your team must hear from you that their work is valuable and appreciated but when they begin to hear it from other departments and outside the organization it will allow them to operate with a higher intrinsic motivation to continue to give one hundred percent.

Let us begin to see the magic of effective leaders starting with our ability to *Listen*. When we begin to listen to those we lead or manage we awaken the voices of those who perhaps feel silenced. Their voices will take you in directions where your own innovation has stalled.

Leaders who don't listen will eventually be surrounded by people who have nothing to say.

—Andy Stanley

We have but two ears and one mouth so that we may listen twice as much as we speak.

—Thomas Edison

Chapter One—Listen

ACCORDING to Swiss psychologist, Jean William Fritz Piaget, there are four stages of cognitive development which are sensorimotor, preoperational, concrete operational, and formal operational. During the time of his research there were many misconceptions about children, such as they were less intelligent than adults. However, his research debunked this myth and found that children simply think, and process information differently as opposed to the preconceived notion that they are inherently less intelligent.

I imagine readers might question my approach of interjecting Piaget in a chapter about listening, but I believe his research undergirds the science of active listening. For those who have raised children or been around a young developing child, we inherently know the importance of listening and while many of us are not fond of a temper tantrum it often is a direct reflection of a child's inability to consider the feelings of others as they are highly egocentric.

Active listening requires the listener to engage with the person speaking empathetically. However, it also requires the listener to make sense of the nonverbal cues the speaker is conveying. When we are raising children or even as we engage our domestic pets we rely heavily upon the nonverbal. Does the screeching cry of a two-month-old mean that they are hungry, in need of a diaper change, or in pain? When our pooch is licking their paw and whimpering, does it mean they are hurt or performing a habitual act? As a leader we must listen with a great deal of empathy as it allows us to hear from our team through the prism of their emotions and perspective. Thus, being an active listener is not just hearing the words being spoken but making sense of what is not being said. No one in good conscious would vehemently scream at their two-month-old because they are demanding attention. Thus, a great leader is always attempting to listen to their staff as they see them not as mere subordinates but as a crucial piece to ensuring the mission and vision are continually seen as the lifeline of their performance. I am reminded of a situation between a supervisor and a manager.

The supervisor has several direct reports who manage the daily operations of the company. Each of the direct reports are equal in their titles and have comparable salaries. However, one of the managers believes they are being treated unfairly as it relates to the delegation of responsibilities. The manager spoke directly to the supervisor and asked why they were given more tasks compared to their counterparts. The manager responded with an extreme level of hostility and reprimanded the supervisor in front of their peers and customers. As a result, of this interaction the manager scheduled a meeting with their supervisor's boss and instead of listening to their concerns the higher-ranking employee constantly interrupted the manager and ultimately sided with the supervisor. This is a classic example of poor active listening skills and exemplifies a leadership team that lacks emotional intelligence.

Oxford Languages defines emotional intelligence as, "the capacity to be aware of, control, and express one's emotions, and to handle interpersonal relationships judiciously and empathetically." When leaders operate with a high level of emotional intelligence, they can handle relationships without causing them to become irreparably damaged. In this scenario the supervisor paid little to no attention to the manager's complaint but instead attacked their character which created a toxic work environment. Great leaders are often faced with untrue claims and those found to be true, but in either situation a great leader will always listen without interrupting and attempt to resolve the situation in the least disruptive manner. This is perhaps why some people shy away from being a leader, as we all know it has some inherent levels of responsibility that require us to be levelheaded.

While Piaget explained the egocentric nature of a child, it is evident these behaviors can also appear in adults, and we must be careful to address them fairly and with emotional intelligence to ensure we do not create a work culture that becomes intolerable to listen to its workers. Thus, listening is an essential habit that all great leaders possess not because it is in the *Harvard Business Review* or appears on the Forbes top ten list of skills held by Fortune 100 Leaders, but because it is impossible to lead a team with inferior listening skills. Great leaders understand that listening is the first step to becoming an effective leader. They equally understand the importance to *Educate* themselves and their teams. The fact that our worlds are interconnected in a global economy makes education essential. Thus, great leaders strategically utilize education so that they can be agile enough to anticipate change and be proactive.

Leadership and learning are indispensable to each other.
—John F. Kennedy

All leaders are learners. The moment you stop learning, you stop leading. I learn as much as I can, from as many as I can, as often as I can.

—Rick Warren

Chapter Two—Educate

NELSON Mandela stated, "Education is the most powerful weapon which you can use to change the world." I believe great leaders strategically use education to change the world and as a matter of circumstance their teams. It has been widely reported that billionaire businessman Warren Buffett spends nearly six hours a day reading according to the Financial Post. Buffett is the 10th richest person in the world, and some might wonder why, he at 91 years young, would spend such an absorbent amount of time reading. The answer is simple, education which we can term as learning is a fluid and a continual process. Leaders who operate with a high level of stagnation often foster a culture of less productive and unmotivated employees.

In higher education and in the corporate sector we often hear professional development tossed around like a frisbee but what does professional development add to the culture of work? Professional development is the ability for an employee to improve their skills by attending a conference, hosting a talk, or reading literature that will inform their current role or future aspirations. Great leaders intrinsically know how to maximize professional development and those leaders with an abundant cash flow ensure their employees are well trained experts in their respective roles.

Professional development is not a chance to secure a vacation at the expense of your employer, and for those employees who utilize it as such, will ultimately learn it is at the expense of their career advancement. Thus, great leaders set a standard of expectations to ensure those employees who seek company sponsored forms of professional development add value to the organization upon their return to the office. I would contend it is not enough to just report your learnings to the team but to find a creative way to implement your learnings in your daily activities. This professional maneuver allows the employee to educate themselves and their colleagues; it signals to the entire organization that you are committed to continual improvement. For example, in higher education there are annual conferences, and many departments support their staff given there is sufficient funding.

While attending a conference, I was most impressed with an attendee who was attempting to address the poor enrollment numbers for African American males. They had come to the conference with a great deal of what I would call prework, as they were aware of the national numbers indicating an alarming decline in African American male enrollment. As we conversed, I soon learned that they headed a program that aimed to attract minority students to their campus. Although they had only been in their role for a year, they were deeply concerned why the program seemed to lose nearly a third of its population.

Throughout the conference, I noticed this person at more than three presentations discussing access and equity on predominantly white college campuses. My intrigue prompted me to exchange contact information and follow-up with the conference attendee. I soon learned that upon their return they provided a presentation to their entire departmental staff and during the next recruiting cycle incorporated some of the techniques used to attract and retain minority students, especially those who self-identified as male and African American.

This employee did not use her time at the conference to meet with distant friends and engage in a continual happy hour, but they were intentional in their effort to seek and implement their learning. It is important to note that is certainly okay to enjoy your personal time at a conference or a company sponsored event however you deem appropriate, given it does not serve as a direct conflict to your respective company or institution. However, you should be excited to bring back the information you have learned and find ways to allow it to inform your work. Great leaders will always support professional development and will fight for funding when it is scarce, but they will equally encourage their team to read, listen to relevant podcast, or meet with an expert to inform their work and to improve the overall competencies of the team.

When you approach your manager or supervisor's office you will not see their Amazon cart or their social media account but will see them looking at trends, reading reports, and developing strategies to improve performance. These, my friends, are the signs of a great leader who is inextricably tied to the desire to educate themselves and those they lead. So, we see a great leader actively listens and educates but beyond these two critical attributes they must be willing to *Act* with a sense of confidence and pragmatism.

Eugene L. Moore

Courageous leaders face unpleasant and even devastating situations with equanimity, then act firmly to bring good from trouble, even if their action is unpopular. Leadership always faces natural inertia and opposition. But courage follows through with a task until it is done.
—*J. Oswald Sanders*

When the time for action arrives, stop thinking and go in.
—*Andrew Jackson*

Chapter Three—Act

IT is true that when you are in a leadership role everyone is looking to you for answers and if you are honest with yourself this level of pressure can cause your leadership approach to be compromised especially if you are hesitant to act. A leader that is deliberate in their actions will likely earn the respect and trust of their peers and those that they lead. The actions a leader takes are often under the highest level of scrutiny but when they incorporate the input from their employees their decisions will be known to be well vetted and sound. There will be times in which decisions will have to be made with little to no input from others but if you have built a strong reputation and trust among your staff such decisions will be generally supported.

Great leaders understand that having complete consensus in a group is unlikely, but they make sure everyone is heard and understands the final position. A great leader is never pretentious or all-knowing but relies heavily on their instincts and willingness to learn from their failures. One of the biggest roles of a leader is to make decisions where some are easy, and others are tough. The late founder of Apple, Steve Jobs, had this approach when making decisions:

> You can't connect the dots looking forward; you can only connect them looking backwards. So, you have to trust that the dots will somehow connect in the future. You have to trust in something-your gut, destiny, life, karma, whatever. This approach has never let me down, and it has made all the difference in my life.

Jobs provided some compelling insights as he offered some anxiety relief to those leaders who believe all of their decisions need to lead toward a favorable outcome. In fact, some of the decisions great leaders make initially seem to fail but it is the leader's ability to assess outcomes and recalibrate, when necessary, that allows them to garner invaluable lessons from their failures. Several years ago, I recall hearing a personal account of a leader who was poorly viewed by their staff.

This leader had an extremely autocratic leadership style, and his team despised their all-knowing and do as I say approach. Overtime, the team became silent and often provided little to no feedback when asked for their insights. The leader had lost all the respect of their staff and began to experience high levels of turnover. The irony of the situation was that the leader felt their woes were largely due to their staff having a poor work ethic and an inability to follow rules. Consequently, the leader ultimately was terminated, but their actions caused major harm to the organization and although many years have since passed, the department still struggles to rewrite the wrongs of their former leader.

We often hear about the success stories of Jobs, Bezos, Sara Blakely, and others but it is important to understand the residual effects of poor leadership. A leader that creates a toxic environment sometimes is unaware of their actions because their leadership style proved to be effective in their previous work environment. Therefore, it is important to always interrogate your leadership style and approach to determine if it is palatable to your new role.

Your actions as a leader will either motivate or discourage your team to be innovative and open to change. Your ability to act firmly in times of prosperity and trouble will create a work culture that will ride the waves of uncertainty. It is simply phenomenal to have a team that supports your leadership; it allows you to enter the room with credibility and whether you have exciting or disheartening news your team will be unwavering in their support. You should want others to say that as a leader, you are not afraid to act and be deliberate and steadfast in your approach. Circumstances are inherently unpredictable and throughout your tenure your team will be able to assess the effectiveness of your decisions. If most of your team support, your ability to act soundly and judiciously you will not have to contend with the consequences of not being valued in your role. As you can see great leaders listen, educate, and act but these habits alone will not be sufficient if a leader lacks the ability to skillfully and equitably *Delegate* tasks.

The Language of Leaders

Strategy equals execution. All the great ideas and visions in the world are worthless if they can't be implemented rapidly and efficiently. Good leaders delegate and empower others liberally, but they pay attention to details, every day.

—*Colin Powell*

No person will make a great business who wants to do it all himself or get all the credit.

—*Andrew Carnegie*

Chapter Four—Delegate

GREAT leaders are masters at delegation and understand their mission and vision is not intended to be a one-person operation. A leader attempts to understand the talents and needs of their team. It is important to know who is the most innovative, who is willing to take initiative, which members are analytical, who is combative, or perhaps who has the most polished presentation skills. Understanding these attributes of your team members allows you to delegate tasks efficiently and effectively. However, it is equally important to know how to motivate your staff to go outside of their comfort zones to foster a culture of growth and learning.

Elon Musk is a prominent figure in business and is largely known for his affiliation with Tesla. He holds a Bachelor of Science degree in business and a Bachelor of Arts degree in physics. Although, he pursued a Ph.D. in materials science at Stanford University he dropped out to focus on his entrepreneurial interests. The purpose of talking about Musk is to show that while he is the CEO of Tesla and named the second richest man in the world, he alone could not have acquired this level of success single-handedly. He not only needed to secure investors, engineers, legal support, a brilliant marketing team, and countless others to make his dreams materialize but he had to empower them to do the work in which he alone is incapable.

We often idolize successful people regardless of their industry affiliation, but one great individual is often surrounded by a great team. For example, Michael Jordan arguably had the greatest talent, but he also had an agent, a spokesperson, an accountant, a coach, teammates, the Chicago Bulls organization, and others who supported his leadership. The reality is that Michael Jordan would not have won 6 NBA championships unless he learned how to pass the ball. Delegation is truly a key component to making a great leader. However, you must ensure delegation does not feel like you are passing on the work to your team while you stand idle not offering any form of support.

I have worked with countless colleagues who are content with watching others work but are quick to take credit for outcomes in which they offered little to no support. These realities create tensions in work groups and is even more detrimental when the behavior is exhibited by the leader. Organizations that experience poor organizational health due to an unfair distribution of work inevitably cause friction and dampen morale. I am reminded of a time in which I was responsible for planning a large-scale company event with the support of a six-figure budget. When I was charged with planning the event I was beyond excited and quickly wanted to conduct a survey to assess how we could improve the event. The survey was telling an indicated many of the employees felt the social activities were boring and could not attract a robust crowd. As a result, I created several activities ranging from an indoor horse race to live karaoke to a live auction.

The event was a glaring success but not because I was spectacular but because I knew the talents of the team. I had an employee who shows horses for a living to call the mock horse race and serve as an auctioneer for the live auction. Not to mention working with the support staff to secure reasonable vendors. The entire event team was comprised of twelve members and if I had not properly delegated tasks, we would have not garnered such success.

Although cliché, a productive and diverse team can often produce greater outcomes than an individual. Great leaders are always looking to delegate and empower their team to get the job done. As you can see a great leader listens, educates, acts, and delegates effectively to propel their team to greater heights but they are always looking for ways to *Excite* their team. Great leaders intrinsically know that where there is great excitement there is often great outcomes.

Eugene L. Moore

Leaders are visionaries. They see the outcome. Leaders are communicators. They tell us what they're seeing. They hold the dream, letting us feel that it's possible. Our minds open up to what they show us could be. We dream with them. We get excited with them, drawing on all our abilities to create the future.
—*Susan Collins*

A leader's role is not to control people or stay on top of things but rather to guide, energize, and excite.

—*Jack Welch*

Chapter Five—Excite

THE ability to excite your team is extremely important especially in a time when competitors are looking to poach the most talented individuals. An effective leader enters the room with the sure desire to figure out new ways in which to motivate their team. Companies like Google, Procter & Gamble, Disney, Chevron, Salesforce, Cisco, and many more are committed to ensuring their employees are highly motivated and excited to work for their respective companies. LinkedIn is inundated with young millennials posting their new positions with these and other top ranked companies. However, excitement is not only a reality for Fortune 100 companies but can be actualized in a small non-profit or in a local independent business.

The desire to spark excitement is in the toolkit of any effective leader. Having worked for a Fortune 5 company and serving as a consultant for a family owed business, I am certain that creating excitement around the mission and vision is an effective strategy to inspire employees to offer their best selves when completing their assigned duties. Famed NFL coach Vincent Lombardi once stated, "Every job is a self-portrait of the person who did it. Autograph your work with excellence." I contend that it is rather difficult to produce excellence without excitement. Hence, I am reminded of a manager who worked for a mid-sized company where the employees had to do menial tasks and for many of them it was their second or third job. As might be expected these workers had low energy and were less motivated to perform their tasks with excellence. Due to the nature of the tasks, it was important to have a sufficient level of detail orientation as there were multiple steps to ensure the process was complete.

Overall, the workers produced quality work, but their efficiency was subpar. The manager quickly observed the need to be more productive and joined the workers in the process and asked what they believed would improve production. The manager received a variation of responses, but the consensus was that the workers believed the workload was too strenuous. The manager quickly demonstrated a new approach to the work and asked the workers to try the new approach. The new approach improved production drastically and as a show of appreciation the manager ordered pizza for the entire crew. The manager also provided a weekly goal and if the team met the objective, they would have a scheduled food day. These small changes helped to improve production but more importantly provided a greater sense of excitement about the work. Most people do not work in Silicon Valley and can proudly say they are a Googler, but many workers are working in low-wage jobs, and they too need to be excited about coming to work.

During the early days of Walmart, Sam Walton would have his signature Saturday morning meeting to excite his associates and provided them with updates about the business. Although the meetings were optional, he wanted his associates to have a since of ownership and rally behind his mission to beat the competition in sales. The associates were not just speaking with their direct supervisor but were getting valuable time with the founder of the company which hopefully translated to a greater sense of self-efficacy.

As a leader Sam Walton in 1962 understood the importance of exciting his employees. In modern day the need to excite employees is even more necessary than before as workers are more transient and less loyal. As you can see a great leader listens, educates, acts, delegates and excites their employees but as Sam Walton demonstrated, employees desire for their leaders to *Reflect* the values they wish to see in their employees. Hence, Sam was up every Saturday morning with his workers who ironically sacrificed time with their families to fulfill the dreams of the Walton family.

When you are in a small boat, you can see who is paddling hard and who's looking around.

—*E.V. Williams*

What you do has far greater impact than what you say.

—*Stephen Covey*

Chapter Six—Reflect

AS a leader it becomes quickly obvious that you are always being watched by everyone. It is never enough to just impress your superiors, but you must work to build trust among all your stakeholders. The old proverb, "Do as I say, not as I do" should have no place in leadership yet there are some leaders who lead their teams with this dangerous mindset. As a culture that loves its celebrities we are always taken aback when a high-profile celebrity falls from grace. While most of us do not have a personal relationship with Kylie Jenner, Kanye West, or Oprah Winfrey we do have a professional relationship with our leaders. In fact, your boss is somewhat of a celebrity. The paparazzi are those who hover around the breakroom spreading unverified gossip, while the workers secretly troll the leader's social media platforms, and yes, some hope for a scandal of some sorts.

If leaders are more conscious of this perceived reality perhaps, they would be more careful with their actions. However, great leaders aim to be authentic and for those who believe that they can dupe their teams, it is highly unlikely. A great leader learns how to deflect attention from themselves to their workers. The leader reflects the values that they desire to see in others and empowers their team to be committed to excellence. When a person is locked into their purpose, they have little to no time to interrogate their boss. A great leader creates a culture of shared vision and responsibility which reduces the room to criticize because that criticism is never one directional within a highly functional team.

A high functioning team is comprised of individual leaders who operate with a standard of accountability. Members of a high-functioning team are less apt to say our leader is the reason for our failed approach, but they think introspectively to discover meaningful solutions. A great leader encourages the forming of highly functional teams and provides clear direction to ensure the objectives are being achieved. They are always ready to step in and offer support, but they are confident in the competence of their team.

An effective leader is inherently a visionary and works tirelessly to get their followers excited about doing the purposeful work, but they unequivocally understand the importance of reflecting the behaviors in which they hope to see in their teams. For instance, I am reminded of a young woman who was a cashier for a major big box grocery chain whose story I will share with you all.

The newly hired employee was returning to work after having been on maternity leave. She was a responsible employee and never missed work. However, one day she missed her bus and arrived to work seventeen minutes late. As she entered the store, she frantically hurried to the back to clock in and as she was leaving to go to the register her supervisor said, "hey, we needed you seventeen minutes ago, don't make this a habit." Despondent by their remarks, she quickly murmured, "sure." As her shift ended, she was clearly still shaken by the comment as this was the first time in six months that she had ever been late but what bothered her the most was the hypocrisy. Her supervisor was habitually late, and everyone knew that they also battled alcoholism as the supervisor was off for two months in rehab. The worker was never late again but eventually resigned and began working for another store but on her last day her supervisor said, "We hate to see you go, you are our best cashier." The cashier smiled and said, "You never made me feel like I was."

This scenario exemplifies the importance of reflecting the behaviors you wish to see in others coupled with the importance of leading with empathy. I am unsure of what happened to the supervisor, but that young woman rose through the ranks to become one of the leading store managers in her district. When we reminisce about her days as a cashier, she is always so humbled and thankful because she believes that her former supervisor showed her how not to lead. Great leaders will work tirelessly to perform their job with integrity, build trust, empower their teams, and reflect an image they desire to see in others. As this book ends, we have learned great leaders, listen, educate, act, delegate, excite, and reflect the values and image of the desired behavior they want from their teams, but you cannot be a great leader if you are unwilling to be a *Showoff* for your team.

Brag about what your people and team are doing. Build them up and help them find their voice.
—*Stephanie Matthews*

You need to be aware of what others are doing, applaud their efforts, acknowledge their successes, and encourage them in their pursuits. When we all help one another, everybody wins.
—*Jim Stovall*

Chapter Seven—Showoff

OXFORD Languages defines a showoff as, "A person who acts pretentiously or publicly parades themselves, their possessions, or their accomplishments." It seems for a leader to possess such a trait would be counterproductive to the success of the organization or team, but such an assertion would be untrue especially when the leader is strategically showing off the talents of their team. When we truly think about the concept of work it seems like an inherently contentious partnership.

In my opinion, the greatest asset to humanity is not one of the natural resources like water or oxygen, although without water or oxygen humans would cease to exist, but for me it is time because once used- it can never be replenished. When I think of work or a career, I see it as a contractual agreement. How much is an employer willing to pay for your time, talent, and resources? Conversely, what do you perceive to be your value and what level of compensation are you willing to accept to relinquish your greatest asset of time? These questions are often hashed out when an offer is extended to a prospective hire but the mere notion, I am sacrificing my greatest asset can be unnerving. Given that this weird agreement has transpired with a worker and an employee, a great leader knows how to finesse this inherently awkward relationship and inspire people to stand behind the mission. Thus, it is imperative for a great leader to ensure all their employees feel valued and are compensated equitably.

Showing off your team is a sure way of acknowledging the team's contributions to other valuable members of the organization. Allow others in the room to feel your excitement as you explain your team's mission and progress. It is clearly not meant to be pretentious but to showcase the talent of your team. Perhaps it is fitting for the Executive Vice President of Sales to know that your team has exceeded sales projections and the strategy they utilized to accomplish their goals. It would be beyond rewarding if while having lunch one of your team members is approached by an executive asking if they are on a particular team and say that you all are doing a phenomenal job with the new sales launch. If your team has an "us versus them" mentality, their performance will always suffer. Great leaders want their employees to be committed and inspired to get the job done with excellence. I am reminded of a seasoned employee who was assigned a particular project to improve the outcomes of students.

This employee went above and beyond to create a manual to help students navigate college. The manual was equipped with the latest research on student retention and provided useful tools to assist students with some of the known barriers to success. The manual received great praise departmentally and had the ability to become a campus wide resource for students. Unbeknownst to the employee, the supervisor expressed their excitement about the manual to their superiors and provided a nomination for them to receive a campus award.

The behavior demonstrated by the supervisor was to showcase the amazing talent of their team. To some it might appear as bragging but when does offering the truth become mistaken as being braggadocios. It is important for leaders to have a winning attitude and openly celebrate victories as well as scrutinize the times in which the goal was not achieved. If both are done professionally employees will be able to handle tough conversations because they trust your leadership. Contrary to what some might believe there is nothing wrong with being a showoff for your team.

If your actions inspire others to dream more, learn more, do more and become more, you are a leader.
—*John Quincy Adams*

Great leaders desire more than a C-Suite position and realize that leading people takes a considerable amount of courage but the reward of empowering others to reach their greatest potential is priceless. Naturally, great leaders will always produce other leaders not just mere fans or followers.
—*Dr. Eugene L. Moore, MBA*

Conclusion

THE word leader is tossed around like a beach ball and many people cannot always articulate what a great leader exemplifies. However, I contend having read this book you are more certain what a leader should have readily accessible in their leadership toolkit. We learned why it is important to *Listen* to your team. We understand the importance of listening as it relates to our partners, children, and friends but as a leader it is just as important if not more critical to listen to those we lead.

As a parent you have an intimate relationship with your children which allows them to listen to your instruction more readily. This level of intimacy must be formed around the mission and values of the company because your team should never walk through the doors for you, but for something that is far greater than even your leadership. Having a strong commitment to *Educate* yourself and others will always keep the train moving. Professional development when utilized strategically keeps your team agile which will allow them to respond to uncertainties. Demonstrating the ability to *Act* with deliberation is critical to a leader's success. Your team needs to be assured you are not hesitant in your decision making nor are you passive. Having a resolute approach that incorporates transparency will allow your team to align with your vision more.

A leader must strategically *Delegate* tasks to ensure their team is operating with a high level of efficiency and effectiveness. The leader must be able to accurately assess the talent on their team and delegate tasks accordingly. It makes absolutely no sense to frustrate your team by assigning tasks that are outside of their ability. To *Excite* your team is to ignite your team to be motivated to get the job done. I would venture to say that most people want to be on a winning team and great leaders know how to craft winning teams. Those that lack focus and excitement typically do not fare well amid challenges but those that are excited are often well positioned to tackle any obstacle. Leaders who *Reflect* the values, work ethic, and expectations they have of their team can produce successful outcomes. The late great Kobe Bryant said in an interview why he does not pass the ball:

I see dudes walk into practice 10 minutes before

practice, and they leave right after. Why the f___ am I gonna pass them the basketball? I don't respect their work ethic. I'm in here busting my a-- every day trying to perfect my craft, and these dudes don't wanna work on their games. I don't trust them. So, I'm not gonna pass them the basketball.

Kobe Bryant reflected the greatness he desired to see in his teammates and any great leader does not hesitate to be an example of excellence. The last piece needed to be a great leader is your ability to respectfully *Showoff* your team's talents and abilities. Your team needs to always know you are in meetings singing their praises. These seven attributes will allow you to boldly speak the language of a leader. Ask yourself, "do I possess the language of a leader?" If the answer is yes, then that is great and if it is no do not be discouraged because not all leaders are born leaders but thankfully many are created, so learn a new language. A language of leaders which will surely provide you and those you lead a roadmap toward excellence.

LET'S GO!

About the Publisher

Let us bring your story to life! Life to Legacy offers the following publishing services: manuscript development, editing, transcription services, ghostwriting, cover design, copyright services, ISBN assignment, worldwide distribution, and eBooks.

Throughout the entire production process, you maintain control over your project. Even if you have no manuscript, we can ghostwrite your story for you from audio recordings or legible handwritten documents. Whether print-on-demand or trade publishing, we have publishing packages to meet your needs. We make the production and publishing processes easy.

We also specialize in family history books so you can leave a written legacy for your children, grandchildren, and others. You put your story in our hands, and we'll bring it to literary life!

Please visit our website:
www.Life2Legacy.com
Or call us at:
877-267-7477
You can also e-mail us at:
Life2Legacybooks@att.net

www.ingramcontent.com/pod-product-compliance
Lightning Source LLC
Chambersburg PA
CBHW031657040426
42453CB00006B/334